Issues in th~ ~

selected and written b~

Contents

Introduction	2
Circus Headlines	6
Letters to a Newspaper	8
Circus Poster	11
Banning Performing Animals: For and Against	12
Circus Spectators	14
My Mother Saw a Dancing Bear (Charles Causley)	16
The Puppy Which Was Put Out For the Dustman	18
Don't Leave Me ...	22
Why Do Animals Get Abandoned?	24
RSPCA Facts And Figures	27
The Fox Cub That Was Saved By a PC's Helmet	28
More About Copper	31
A Killer Lies (Benjamin Zephaniah)	35
Fox Hunting: For and Against	38
Don't Feed the Birds – Please	41
Letter From the Birds	43
Feeding Wild Birds	46
Take Not Away (John Dryden)	48

Introduction

This book deals with four issues concerning animal welfare which are often in the news:
- **Performing animals**
- **Abandoning animals**
- **Fox hunting**
- **Feeding birds**

People use animals in different ways: for example, we keep them as pets, use them for work (e.g. police horses and sniffer dogs), sport (e.g. racing and hunting), entertainment (e.g. circuses and films), advertising, research and, of course, food and clothing.

3

Animals can bring a great deal of pleasure into our lives, along with a fascination with the way they look, behave and live. Most people would never deliberately harm them.

However, there are those who are cruel to animals in some way. Cruelty to animals can take many forms. For example:
- deliberately hurting them
- neglecting and not caring for them properly
- being ignorant about how to care for them
- damaging their natural environments and habitats
- not treating them as beings with their own feelings and emotions

It can be argued that some forms of cruelty are worse than others – that harming animals through ignorance is not as bad as harming them deliberately. But if an animal suffers in both cases, is there really a difference?

Letters to a Newspaper

Dear Sir

When a well-known animal trainer from a famous circus family is found guilty of cruelty to animals, it is inevitable that feelings will run high. Who would not be distressed by video clips of animals being beaten? Who would not feel an immediate burst of sympathy with those who say that the only way to protect circus animals is to have a complete ban on all animal acts?

I am a passionate believer in Animal Rights. We have a responsibility to treat all animals not only with compassion but also with dignity. However, I am also a passionate believer in the rights of the individual. Should we deny out of hand the right of our children to be enchanted by prancing horses or majestic elephants? Surely it is not impossible to ensure that animals who are kept for performing are treated and trained with kindness and sympathy? Then we might have the best for animals and for children.

Fair-minded, Slough

Dear Sir

Fair-minded of Slough is not fair-minded at all: he or she is simply woolly minded. We live in a real world and no matter what laws and procedures are in place to ensure the welfare of animals, as the recent case has shown, those laws will always be broken and animals will suffer as a result. A complete ban on circus animals is the only answer.

Realist, Bristol

P.S. How would Fair-minded fancy prancing around a circus ring with a whip to the back of his/her legs?

Banning Performing Animals: For and Against

The case for:

- **Training animals to perform tricks is unnatural and does not show them the respect they deserve.**
- **Methods of training involving force and punishment are cruel.**
- **Many people do not like watching circus animals. Circuses can be just as successful without animal acts.**
- **Some circus animals are healthy and well-treated, some are not. A ban on animal acts is the only way to protect them all.**

The case against:

- **Tricks like jumping through hoops or a sea-lion balancing a ball are based on an animal's natural behaviour.**
- **Animals can be trained with patience and bribery (giving tit-bits and praise as a reward). There is no need for any cruelty.**
- **Many people want to see acts which feature animals not simply those with people performing.**
- **Animals in captivity can become ill if they are bored. Performing can prevent this.**

Circus Spectators

I sat there absolutely spellbound. I held my breath and could not believe that I was watching the powerful rippling muscles of a real-life tiger as it performed just yards in front of me in the ring. The relationship between beast and trainer was a special one and I felt privileged to witness the animal's beauty at such close quarters.

I grew increasingly uncomfortable as I watched the tiger, this powerful animal reduced to the level of a plaything. Such majesty deserves the freedom of its natural habitat – not the confines of a sawdust ring and a strutting, so-called trainer.

My Mother Saw a Dancing Bear

My mother saw a dancing bear
By the schoolyard, a day in June.
The keeper stood with chain and bar
And whistle-pipe, and played a tune.

And bruin lifted up its head
And lifted up its dusty feet,
And all the children laughed to see
It caper in the summer heat.

They watched as for the Queen it died.
They watched it march. They watched
  it halt.
They heard the keeper as he cried,
"Now, roly-poly!" "Somersault!"

And then, my mother said, there came
The keeper with a begging-cup,
The bear with burning coat of fur,
Shaming the laughter to a stop.

They paid a penny for the dance,
But what they saw was not the show;
Only, in bruin's aching eyes,
Far-distant forests, and the snow.

Charles Causley

The puppy which was put out for the dustman

by KATE HURRY

AT ONLY eight weeks old, she was as unwanted as the heap of rubbish she was trapped in. Cowering in a cardboard box, the abandoned collie almost succumbed to the winter cold at the side of the road.

But then fate intervened in the form of a neighbour. As the woman went to put her bin out for the dustmen, she saw the box move. "She thought it was a frog at first," RSPCA inspector Nigel Shelton said yesterday. "She couldn't believe her eyes when she discovered an eight-week-old collie."

A week on, Lilly – as Mr Shelton has

Abandoned

Lilly and Nigel Shelton

called her – is about to be adopted by a new family. And her story is being used to reinforce the RSPCA's campaign against buying pets as Christmas gifts. As part of that drive, the animal charity persuaded BBC TV's Animal Hospital to come and film her recovery.

Mr Shelton, 28, whose beat includes Cheshunt in Hertfordshire where Lilly was found, called her dumping a "sickening" act.

Had she not been discovered when she was, he said, she would certainly have died. "With it being cold, she would have just gone to sleep to try to keep warm," he explained. She would not have woken up again.

Mr Shelton took her to his North London home where she made a full recovery from a fever. Now she will enjoy a warm Christmas after moving in with her new owners later this week.

Don't Leave Me ...

Don't leave me:

I am too young to abandon.

Don't leave me:

I shall be cold and lonely.

Don't leave me:

I shall be frightened and hungry.

Don't leave me:

I may not live without you.

Don't leave me ...
But if you keep me,
Will you care for me?

Will I still be cold and lonely,
Hungry and frightened,
Mistreated and neglected?

Leave me.
Perhaps then I might survive?

Wendy Body

Why Do Animals Get Abandoned?

Pets are not toys – you can't simply put them away in a cupboard when the novelty of having them wears off. Pets need time, money and willingness to care for them.

There are many reasons why pets are abandoned. For example:
- The owners get fed up with looking after them.
- They grow too big for the owner's home.
- They cost too much money to feed.
- They have too many puppies or kittens.
- The owners want to go on holiday.
- They can't be controlled.

Before anyone gets a pet they should ask themselves:

- Can I be a kind and loving owner?
- Can I afford to feed and care for my pet properly?
- What will happen to my pet when I go on holiday? Is there someone to look after it? Can I afford the cost of a kennels or a cattery?
- Am I prepared to spend time with my pet?
- Do I want my cat/dog to have puppies/kittens? Should I have it neutered?

⚠ **THINK BEFORE YOU GET A PET!**

RSPCA Facts and Figures

In 1997 the RSPCA:
- rescued 8255 stranded or abandoned animals from danger
- found new homes for 70 563 cats and dogs
- investigated 133 664 complaints of cruelty to animals
- was responsible for getting 2650 convictions for cruelty to animals.

The fox cub that was saved by a PC's hel-

by Kate Ginn

EXHAUSTED and badly injured, the fox cub sought refuge in a rabbit hole as the frenzied pack of hounds moved in for the kill.

Huntsmen, bearing down ready to start digging out their quarry, clashed with hunt saboteurs who were attempting to block their way.

Death seemed to be just a matter of minutes away for the fox cowering inside the hole, until an extraordinary gesture from a policeman.

He took off his

On the mend: Copper the fox cub would have died without treatment, said the vet who tended him.

helmet so that it could be used by a saboteur to shield the entrance to the tunnel, to keep the snarling dogs at bay and save the animal's life.

While members of the Sussex's Chidding- ford, Leconfield and Cowdray Hunt backed off, one of the anti-hunt protesters managed to rescue the terrified fox and wrapping him up in a coat, took him away to safety.

DAILY MAIL, 16 FEBRUARY 1999

More about Copper

Copper, as the fox cub who was approximately one-year-old came to be known, was first examined by a vet, Richard Edwards from the Alphapet veterinary clinic near Bognor Regis. The fox had a few bite wounds on his hind legs and was losing a small amount of blood. But the real problem was that he was suffering from severe shock or trauma. Mr Edwards said that he had only ever seen this type of shock in animals involved in road traffic accidents.

Copper responded to treatment very quickly. When first examined he was semi-comatose. Within two hours he

was sitting up and looking around. Within eight hours, said Mr Edwards, he had "chewed his drip out and was quite happy to try and bite me!"

Copper is believed to be the first fox to be examined by a vet after surviving being chased by hounds. The state he was in is being taken as evidence that foxes do suffer severe shock when being chased and hunted.

But people who support hunting have argued that the trauma was caused by Copper being captured and transported into a strange environment rather than by being chased.

However, Richard Edwards does not agree. He said: "I have been examining and treating foxes for over ten years. I find it very hard to believe that this could be the case."

Another expert, Professor Stephen Harris of the Foxwatch Project at Bristol University agrees with this view. The project has handled and transported hundreds of foxes before releasing them again.

After being treated by Richard Edwards, Copper was taken to Hyderstile wildlife hospital in Surrey. There, he was kept and cared for until he could be released back into the wild – when the hunting season would be over.

A Killer Lies

He's a fox hunter, he said
"Foxes need controlling, they
  spread germs
They're always mating."
I think he's exaggerating.
He's a fox hunter, he said
"They're wild animals, they eat lambs
and they eat chickens."
He needs chickens for his kitchen

He calls foxes beast, but he collects their teeth,
He kills thousands every year
Once he whispered in me ear,
"It will kill you with its bite
That is why fox hunting's right,
Can't you sense they are evil
So unlike hunting people,
They are the enemy of our community
I love it when they're caught
And they make such good sport,
I never tasted one
When our hounds get them they're gone,
I am good at this you know
I'm a kind of Hunt hero."

He's a Fox Hunter
His Daddy taught him well
When his hounds scent de smell
Excitement meks him yell,
He's a Fox Hunter
Know him by his killer eyes
Something dead must be his prize
He's de kind dat's **civilised.**

Benjamin Zephaniah

Fox Hunting: For and Against

Pro-hunting arguments

1. Foxes are pests and hunting is a good way to control their numbers.
2. Fox hunting helps farmers who are being pestered by foxes.
3. Foxes kill lambs.
4. Foxes kill chickens.
5. Fox-hunting helps conserve the countryside.
6. Fox hunting is a traditional sport. If fox-hunting was banned, many people would lose their jobs and packs of hounds would have to be destroyed.
7. Foxes do not suffer – they are killed quickly by the hounds.

Anti-hunting responses

1. There are about 250 000 foxes in Britain. Each year 15 000–20 000 are killed by hunting. 50 000–100 000 are killed on the roads. The rural fox population remains fairly stable.
2. Foxes which cause problems to farmers can be humanely shot by experts.
3. Foxes eat rabbits which helps farmers. 0.5%–3% of lambs are killed by foxes compared to 25% that die from starvation, exposure or illness.
4. Chickens are safe if properly fenced in.
5. Wildlife areas are damaged by the hunt passing through them.

6. Hunting can still take place without killing foxes: drag hunting uses a scent laid by a human for the hounds to follow. Fox hunting could be replaced by drag hunting.
7. Recent evidence suggests that foxes do suffer during the chase (see page 33). Anti-hunt supporters say that foxes are not always killed quickly.

DON'T FEED THE BIRDS – PLEASE

by Suzannah Marsh

Well-meaning people are being blamed for Bristol's growing problem with pigeon and seagull droppings.

The birds flock to areas in the city where they can pick up titbits thrown to them.

But the mess they cause creates an expensive headache for companies trying to maintain their offices and councils responsible for statues and monuments.

The droppings are acidic – and can have a similar effect on stone as rust has on metal.

The cost of damage caused by bird mess nationally is put at more than £10 million a year.

Bristol Evening Post, 21 January 1999

Letter From the Birds

Letter which might have been sent in response to the article on pages 41–42:

Sir

We recently came across a copy of the *Bristol Evening Post* under a bench on the Downs. We read the article on pigeon and seagull droppings with great interest.

However, we must take issue with the irresponsible use of the headline: *Don't Feed the Birds – Please*. Our observations lead us to suggest that there are people who only read the headlines in newspapers. Such people could be under the impression that they were being asked to stop feeding ALL wild birds.

Were this to happen, it would be a tragedy. Many wild birds (including, I'm afraid to say, those large greedy pigeons and seagulls) would die of starvation. In winter, many wild birds largely rely on humans to put out food for them. So please tell your readers: DON'T stop feeding the birds!

Yours

A. Sparrow, A. Blackbird,
A. Finch, A. Starling, A. Thrush and Robin Redbreast

Feeding Wild Birds

October is the time when the natural food which birds eat becomes hard for them to find, so this is a good time to start feeding them. Carry on until early summer. Place food out in the open away from trees or bushes where cats can hide.

As well as putting out bird seed, garden birds can be fed with:
- bread – make sure it is not too dry because this will cause dehydration in birds
- peanuts, but NOT salted ones which will also cause dehydration
- potatoes – cooked, not raw!

- cheese – crumbled or grated
- fat – chopped bacon rinds, fat trimmed from meat and suet
- stale cake and biscuits
- cooked rice, pasta and pastry
- fruit, e.g. bruised apples or pears.

Birds need water all the year round – not only to drink but also to bathe. Having their feathers clean and in good condition helps birds to keep warm in winter.

Change the water to keep it clean – and free of ice in winter.

Take Not Away

**Take not away the life you cannot give,
For all things have an equal right to live.**

John Dryden (1631–1700)